W9-BQM-346

Christianity Made Simple Series

Christianity Made Simple: Belief *is the first in a*
series of books which will cover some main themes of the
Christian faith. Other projected volumes include:
Christianity Made Simple: Ethics
Christianity Made Simple: Jesus
Christianity Made Simple: Bible

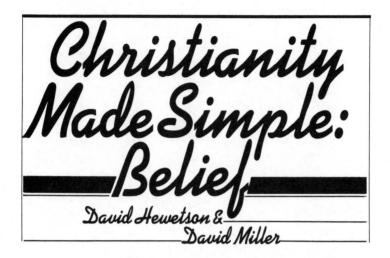

Christianity Made Simple: Belief

David Hewetson & David Miller

InterVarsity Press
Downers Grove
Illinois 60515

© Albatross Books, 1983.

Printed in America by InterVarsity Press, Downers Grove, Illinois, with permission from Albatross Books, Sutherland, Australia.

InterVarsity Press is the book-publishing division of Inter-Varsity Christian Fellowship, a student movement active on campus at hundreds of universities, colleges and schools of nursing. For information about local and regional activities, write IVCF, 233 Langdon St., Madison, WI 53703.

Distributed in Canada through InterVarsity Press, 860 Denison St., Unit 3, Markham, Ontario L3R 4H1, Canada.

ISBN 0-87784-811-4

Printed in the United States of America

Library of Congress Cataloging in Publication Data

Hewetson, David.
    Christianity made simple—belief.

    (Christianity made simple series)
    1. Theology, Doctrinal—Popular works.   I. Miller,
David.   II.   Title.   III.   Title: Belief.
IV.   Series.
BT77.H485   1983   230   83-10866
ISBN 0-87784-811-4

---

15   14   13   12   11   10   9   8   7   6   5   4   3   2   1
94   93   92   91   90   89   88   87   86   85   84   83

Contents

Introduction

HI !

K

We have decided to use the title *Christianity made simple* for this series, though we realize this could be misunderstood. Some might think we mean 'Christianity made easy' — and that is impossible! Jesus clearly told us that his disciples must take up the cross, deny themselves and practise radical 'surgery' on anything that stands in the way of entering the kingdom. Christianity can never be made easy.

However the Christian faith can be 'made simple' or at least be simply explained. Of course God's personality must be highly complex, his plans for the world unbelievably intricate, his influence on us mysterious and incredibly subtle. But God himself in his relationships with us is plain and straightforward. Indeed, so simple is his approach to us that, in response, he expects an attitude which Jesus describes as child-like.

The truth about God may have immense intellectual appeal to academic believers — they may ponder it deeply and write great tomes about it. But God's truth comes through just as plainly to unintelligent and uneducated people, to primitives and even to the mentally disabled. *All* may come to know him personally in the simplest and most intimate way. Because we believe this, we have opted for the word 'simple' in our title.

When the subject is the expert

Theology is the 'science' of God. It is the study of his nature, and his relationship to the world and mankind. But as a science or body of systematic thought, theology is not derived from human investigation in the same way as the science of physics, chemistry or astronomy. God is not available to our scrutiny as a piece of natural phenomena, a molecule or a distant star. We cannot 'master' him as one would a problem in the world of the natural sciences.

All our knowledge of God, as we shall see in the first chapter, results from his revealing himself to us. He is the only expert there is on himself. No amount of speculation and thought on our part could possibly yield the truths about himself that he has condescended to show us.

The grouping of these truths into a systematic whole is what theology is all about. Some may wonder why we should do this at all. If God has revealed himself to us, isn't that enough? Why do we also need to systematize the truth about him? Is it possible to do so anyway? Might it not be a hindrance to the simple experience of knowing God — to reduce God to an intellectual equation?

Throughout the centuries Christians have found that without a good theological framework individuals and churches go astray. Their piety and their devotion are not a substitute for an accurate knowledge of God and his purposes. And wrong presuppositions about him soon lead to distorted views on a lot of other things as well.

Theology is rather like a chart or map. It is not the terrain itself, but it is an invaluable guide to finding your way across it. Theology is not God and, if we treat our particular brand of doctrine as 'divine', we shall soon be caught up in a subtle kind of idolatry. No, theology is not God, but it is an essential guide to his nature and ways. Without some theological basis, we will soon lose our way.

We hope this book will help you explore some of the basic ideas about God, the world and yourself. We have selected a number of theological topics which go to the very heart of Christianity. We suggest that you use the book, and the questions at the back, as a basis for discussion with others in mutual discovery of the great truths of God and the Christian life. And remember as you do so that the truths about God are personal, not merely academic. As Jesus put it: 'You will know the truth and the truth will set you free' (John 8:32).

1.
Revelation

How God has shown himself to us

Is there anybody there?

Where is God? We cannot see him; we cannot hear him. Often, when we cry out to him in anguish, no voice answers. Is he there? Why does he not speak to us?

The Christian answer to these riddles is that God *has* revealed himself to us, that he has spoken. But not in a way that allows us to see him physically or hear him audibly. His revelation does not work that way. If God is great and wise — and he could hardly be God if he is not — then he must know the best way to communicate with us. It is not for us to complain that his revelation is not effective. Rather it is for us to learn what sort of communication he has adopted and to respond to it.

Not mankind seeking God, but God seeking mankind

Revelation means to unveil or 'uncover'. In revelation it is God who takes the initiative. He tells us who he is and what he is like, because we cannot work it out for ourselves. We cannot find him by searching, because he is above and beyond us and our puny perceptions. Worse, our real problem is that we do not want to know him at all — at least know him as he really is.

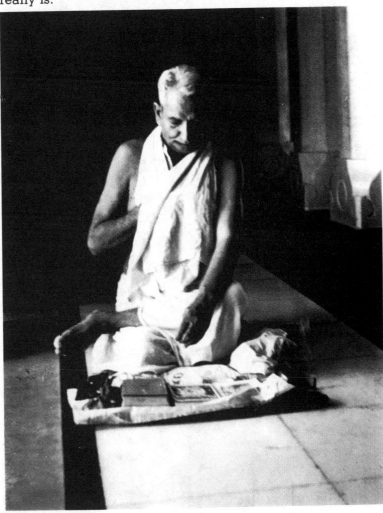

Taming the Almighty

We are more at home with our own ideas about religion — with thoughts which are comfortable and reassuring, with a 'God' who is rather like us and who can be brought into line with our own expectations. This God is domesticated — like a religious 'pet', rather than the wild, untamed presence of the Almighty.

Recipe for confusion

Because human beings differ so much from each other, their ideas about God are very different too and often quite contradictory. Given the fact that we cannot find God for ourselves and that our ideas about him often contradict each other, it is obviously quite impossible to discover God by lumping everyone's religious ideas together, or even by examining them one by one. What we get, in fact, is total religious confusion.

If the real truth about God is to be made known, then it is God himself who must make it known. He must take the initiative. He must reveal, unveil or disclose himself. It is the claim of Christianity that this is exactly what he has done.

Two types of revelation

Revelation takes a number of different forms. Theologians call some revelations 'general' and some 'special'.

1. General revelation

God reveals himself in some ways to all people everywhere. He does this through nature and its testimony, and through human nature itself.

(a) Nature

The created world in all its beauty and complexity declares God's character. It is mute, but it communicates with us in 'sign language'. It informs us that God is the Maker and Master of all things, and that we ought to worship him. The provision of our daily needs is also a witness to God's goodness and concern for us. In other words, in their ordinary daily lives all people everywhere, whether they are consciously listening or not, are being spoken to by God.

(b) Human nature

God's general message is not limited to the natural world outside of us. Our own natures as well are an avenue through which he communicates with us. We were made in God's image or spiritual likeness. Human qualities like personality, rationality and morality reflect the One who implanted them in us. The human conscience, evidence that God's law is 'written on our hearts', is an inner witness to a moral God who created us to be concerned about right and wrong, even though we do not always agree with each other in detail about what things are right and what are wrong. What we *are* is therefore one of the ways by which God speaks to us.

Many people tend to emphasize general or natural (as contrasted with supernatural) revelation. 'We worship God in the great outdoors', they say. 'We are not bound by the doctrines and dogmas of men. We are free to find God in our own way, amid the beauties of nature and in the rich treasures of the human heart.'

But what *do* they learn about God in nature and humanity? That he is there, certainly. That he is wise and powerful, yes. But nature is also cruel and bloodthirsty, deeply committed to its own survival through conflict and through reproduction. If we follow that lead, we shall produce — as the ancient world did — gods which are often cruel and sensual, demanding even human sacrifice.

If we look for God in our own hearts, we may discover concepts of morality and reason. But we will also discover pride, selfishness and a whole menagerie of unpleasantness. Do we want a God like that? It is the Bible which introduces the idea of natural revelation. But the Bible also tells us plainly that, though God uses it to tell us important truths about himself and our responsibilities, it does not give us answers to life's most important questions.

General revelation helps to preserve mankind by giving people some idea of good and evil, truth and falsehood, justice and injustice, thus preventing them from sliding into bestiality. But general revelation cannot help us come to know God as he is, nor rescue us from our self-destructive ways. It can accuse us of breaking God's law written on our hearts, but it cannot offer us forgiveness. And it cannot tell us of God's true nature, of his coming into the world in the person of Jesus Christ, or of his supreme act of liberation through Christ's death and resurrection. For all such essential truths we must turn to God's special revelation of himself.

2. Special revelation

When you take into account the barriers which we have erected against God, it is quite clear that, if he is going to get through to us, he must make a specific and concerted approach: he must give us some form of special revelation.

The Christian claim is that the Bible is the record of how he has done this. It tells us how, through powerful saving actions and the interpretations of these by people whom he called into close fellowship with himself, God has increasingly unveiled the mystery of his being and nature. He showed himself to people in ways that they were able to cope with — in terms of their own time, place and culture.

God continually built on this new understanding until the ground was clear enough for him to make a personal appearance in truly human terms, i.e. in the coming of Jesus.

In the past
God spoke
to our ancestors

many times
and in many ways
through the prophets,
but in these last days
he has spoken to us
through his Son.

Hebrews 1:1-2

Concrete not abstract,
real not imaginary

God's special revelation of himself occurs in history. It is in
this world of space and time, not in some remote ethereal
realm. He unveils himself in the great 'saving events' which
the Bible records, associated with the history of the Hebrew
people. Although this is a carefully selected history, it is not
unconnected with the history of the wider world — with great
world powers like Egypt, Assyria, Persia and Rome.

Words as well as deeds . . .

God came down to save his people and, in saving them, he showed them who he is and what he is like. This special revelation of himself was in *words* as well as actions. He took certain people into his confidence, so that they would be able to understand what was happening and then interpret it to others.

They are the prophets or 'seers' of the Old Testament, whose God-assisted gaze pierced the superficialities of history and perceived God at work. They are the apostles of the New Testament, close companions of Jesus who were also permitted to see things about him which were not available even to the religious 'experts' of the day.

... interpreting the event

These events by themselves would not make sense without words. They need interpretation. Take, for example, the crossing of the Red Sea. To an Egyptian it would have been extraordinary bad luck; to an unbelieving Israelite extraordinary good luck; but to Moses and those who shared his vision it was nothing less than the characteristic action of God. They recognized this event as the work of the One who runs the world and shows mercy and compassion to insignificant people.

Similarly in the New Testament, the apostles saw the real truth about Jesus. They walked and talked with him, sharing his life intimately. They were eye-witnesses of the remarkable events that accompanied his life and his death. Jesus gave them his own Spirit so that they might have a clear and accurate insight into who he really was — the conceptual framework by which to interpret these events. Then he called them to take his revealed insight and share it with the world at large by their preaching and teaching. Fortunately, they also put it into written form.

God's ultimate declaration

God's special revelation climaxes in the person of Jesus. In him, this revelation also comes to a close.

This does not mean that God has nothing further to say to us: it simply means that his revelation of himself in Jesus is so definitive that it becomes the lens through which we now see all other truth about him, ourselves and life in general. It is almost as if we enter a 'time machine' and go backwards in history to the very events that the Bible records. Through the same Spirit that enlightened the prophets and apostles, we can hear God speaking to us through the historical situations of those who first heard the message.

To put it another way, God brings forward to our own time and situation the truths which were revealed and recorded centuries ago. Put it any way you like, it all amounts to the same thing: God speaks to us *now* through his special revelation, the message and person of Jesus.

2.
God

Who God is and what he is like

Defining terms

The first Christians talked a lot about God. But then so did everybody. Jews, Greeks, Romans — they all did a lot of God-talk.

But what each one of them meant by 'God' was very different. And the same is true now. Sometimes people's beliefs about God are no more than what they think is good or important.

Some talk about a 'prime mover' or a 'life force', as if nature itself is God. Others look inward and try to find harmony with the universe through meditation. Still others equate science or evolution with God. Such 'gods', of course, are not personal and will never satisfy our deep need for a personal relationship with the Creator.

Apart from the conspiracy of silence about God today —
people get embarrassed when you mention him — most
people still believe that he exists.

But is what people call 'God' *really* God, or just a projection of
their own thoughts?

For many, there's no contact between them and God. Most
people do nothing about him, or don't even believe that there
is anything to be done. Not knowing who God really is and not
doing anything about it usually go together.

How the first Christians saw God

When the first Christians spoke about God, they meant God the *Invader*. Though he is above and beyond the world, he penetrates every part of it and holds the whole of creation together.

HE'S GOT THE WHOLE WIDE WORLD

Once in history God paid us a person-to-person visit. He invaded his own world!

Now that kind of God is not just our idea. He took the initiative. When a Christian says 'God', that's what he means — he means that the great and mighty, one and only true God was born into our world as Jesus Christ. *That's* what 'God' means.

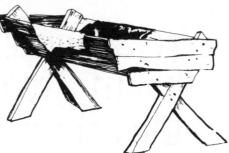

Like your landlord
    becoming your
    tenant:

Like your managing
    director up before
    you for an interview:

Like Beethoven
    lining up for a ticket
    to his own concert:

Like a principal
    having to sit in
    the corner:

Like a good architect
living in a slum
built by a rival:

Like Picasso painting
by numbers:

God lived
among
us.

Goo!

Simon Jenkins,
from his poem 'Like . . .'[1]

A real brain-teaser

No one pretends that this is easy to understand. If Jesus was God, who was running the universe while Jesus was here? Or if God was in heaven and on earth at the same time, are there two gods or has God got a split personality?

When Jesus returned to his Father, he sent his Spirit into the world. This Spirit is also God's Spirit and God. Confusing, isn't it! If Jesus came to *reveal* God to us, why then is it all so complicated?

Two important considerations

1. God can't be easily examined or analysed.

He is not a mathematical problem for which we must find a solution. He is God. He is the Maker and Master of the universe — and maybe other universes as well. For him, light years are just a step and millennia are just a moment. Within himself he must be vastly more complex that we could ever think or imagine.

Could an insect understand a human being? Could an ant understand a galaxy? Can a person comprehend God? The big wonder is that he is so concerned with the human race. His love for us is so intense that he actually became one of us. Now *that* is a miracle — but also a mystery!

This is the kind of God the Scriptures reveal.

The experience of the Apostles was of a personal God. Our explanation of him must correspond with their experience.

2. God's self-revelation must be taken seriously.

The fact that God has revealed himself to us in a three-personal way must not be lightly dismissed. It is not something we could have guessed for ourselves.

God did not try to win us over by watering down the truth about himself. So his tri-unity must be important. Even if some of our descriptions of him are sometimes crude and clumsy, they still give us a true and useful understanding of his real nature.

Some traditional attempts at explaining the Trinity

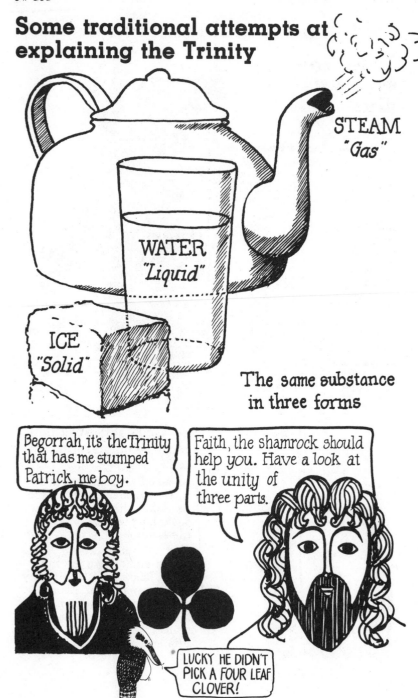

STEAM *"Gas"*

WATER *"Liquid"*

ICE *"Solid"*

The same substance in three forms

Begorrah, it's the Trinity that has me stumped Patrick, me boy.

Faith, the shamrock should help you. Have a look at the unity of three parts.

LUCKY HE DIDN'T PICK A FOUR LEAF CLOVER!

All these examples are useful, but imperfect. If pressed too far, they can even be misleading. For the Christian, the problem is the limitation of words to explain his or her own experience of God and God's revelation in history. The problem is with language, not with the truth that is being expressed by the language.

British theologian, James Packer, has accurately described this particular problem by his use of the word *antinomy*:

> 'The whole point of an antinomy — in theology at any rate — is that it is not a real contradiction, though it looks like one. It is an *apparent* incompatibility between two apparent truths. An antinomy exists when a pair of principles stand side by side, seemingly irreconcilable, yet both undeniable . . . You see that each must be true on its own, but you do not see how they can both be true together . . .
>
> 'Modern physics faces an antinomy, in this sense, in its study of light. There is cogent evidence to show that light consists of waves, and equally cogent evidence to show that it consists of particles. It is not apparent how light can be both waves and particles, but the evidence is there . . . the two seemingly incompatible positions must be held together, and both must be treated as true. Such a necessity scandalizes our tidy minds, no doubt, but there is no help for it if we are to be loyal to the facts.'[2]

Intellectually the Christian accepts the truth about the one God being three-personal, recognizing that God knows more about himself than we do. But, when the Christian does so, he or she discovers that this apparently contradictory description of God makes sense in a number of ways.

Why the doctrine of the Trinity is important

1. It helps us see that God is love.

For love to exist, there must be a lover and a beloved. God, being eternal and self-contained, has always had within himself these two elements. God the Father has loved and given himself to God the Son from before time. And the Son has returned that love from eternity to eternity — including when, in great humility, he was born into the world as Jesus Christ.

God — Father, Son and Spirit — is a fellowship within himself. The central truth of Christianity is that he has condescended to include us in that fellowship.

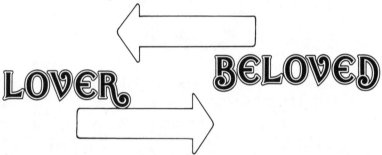

LOVER   BELOVED

2. It helps explain our actual experience of God.

The doctrine of the Trinity is not a riddle worked out by theologians to confuse simple believers — and keep themselves in a job as official explainers. The experience preceded the doctrine. It was the way the first Christians came to know God and have fellowship with him.

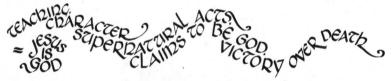

TEACHING CHARACTER SUPERNATURAL ACTS CLAIMS TO BE 'ONE' GOD VICTORY OVER DEATH = JESUS IS GOD

As Jews, they had held doggedly to the great truth that there is only one God. Now the first Christians also became convinced that Jesus too was God. Although Jesus had placed himself under certain limitations in order to live a fully human life, his character, his teaching, his ability to do supernatural things, his claims to be 'one' with his Father and finally his victory over death made them realize they were dealing with no ordinary human being.

3. It helps us understand how God revealed himself in Jesus.

Jesus called himself God's 'only begotten Son', i.e. he was a different person to the Father, but with the same divine nature. Opening their lives to Jesus, the disciples came into a new and intimate relationship with God, so intimate in fact that they learned to call on him as 'Father' in the same way as Jesus did.

4. It helps us understand how the Holy Spirit operates in our lives.

When Jesus was about to leave his disciples, he began to teach them about God's Spirit. The Spirit, he said, would take up permanent residence with them and apply from the 'inside' all that Jesus had done for them. God in heaven, who had become God alongside them, would now become God within them: the Spirit would be like Jesus' other self in their hearts.

And this was, of course, exactly how it turned out for the first Christians. Coming to *God* and trusting in what *Jesus* had done for them on the cross, they experienced God's *Spirit*, who brought a new understanding of truth, a new power to live by and a new desire to become like Jesus.

The doctrine of the Trinity was not a puzzle, but a solution. It was the early Christians' way of expressing who God really is and how they experienced him.

3.
Creation

What nature tells us about God

God the Maker

Traditionally God is described as the 'Maker of heaven and earth'. He made the universe, huge and complex as it is. He made our world, that beautiful and hospitable planet that makes human life possible. He made man — marvellous, creative, capable of such wonderful things, the crown of his creation and the one with whom he shares earthly control.

Matter from mind

God not only formed all things; he actually called into being their very substance. Because he is God — all powerful, all wise, all knowing — his very thoughts and intentions become solid reality. When he says 'Let there be . . .', it actually happens.

All matter comes from his great mind.

Matters beyond our minds

People find it almost impossible to comprehend the vast distances of space. Scientific discovery finds wonder after wonder as men continue to explore the creation. And when we say 'God', we mean the one who made it all and who keeps it all going.

How great, how majestic, how wise, how wonderful he is!

Small minds

Yet many people today walk through God's handiwork with never a thought for him. Or else they get so caught up in what he has made that they take his good gifts and forget the Giver.

Even scientific research becomes so preoccupied with the tangible evidence of his wisdom that it revels in its discoveries for their own sake and honours the created rather than the Creator.

It is almost like analysing a great work of art and scientifically describing its components, but forgetting the one who conveyed its message and invested in it his own personality. It is, in fact, to miss the point altogether.

How the world began

The well-known German theologian and preacher, Helmut Thielicke, advertised a series of sermons on the biblical story of creation. He received a frank letter which said: 'What do you think you know about creation anyhow? Who was there when it happened? After all, there were no reporters there to hear those words, *Let there be!* Yet the Bible acts as if it were presenting an eyewitness account.'

Certainly the only eye that could have witnessed creation is God's eye. He was the only one there when it happened, the only 'reporter' to get the real story of a world being born. It is a great pity that there has often been so much debate about the kind of account of it that he has given to us in the Bible that many people—believers as well as unbelievers—have not stopped to *listen* to what he is saying to us in it.

Whatever the Genesis account is or is not saying, it is God's word to us, telling us important things about him and about ourselves. We are in danger of missing the wood for the trees if we focus too much on the form of the Bible's account of creation and not on its underlying purpose.

The first chapter of the first book of the Bible has God as its subject. He is, in fact, the subject of the whole Bible, but in its first verses he is shown to be the subject of everything and everyone. He is behind the world and the universe, life and human history—he is the foundation upon which it all rests.

Order out of chaos

God *creates* (a verb the Bible uses only of him). He has brought everything into being in a way which is beyond our invention or imitation. In fact the universe is as big a miracle as any other that has ever been performed, though we live so close to it that we often do not recognize it as such. Our familiarity with it robs us of the awe and wonder that we would feel if we had come upon it for the first time.

The order and beauty that we see around us has replaced the emptiness and formlessness of the primeval world. God specializes in bringing order out of disorder, just as Jesus stilled the storm on the Lake of Galilee, calmed the fears in the hearts of his disciples and brought peace and sanity to the mind of the wild man that he met in the tombs on the shore.

Humanity is the crown of God's handiwork. Humanity is part of nature and yet independent of it. Humanity bears a kind of 'family likeness' to God—we are potential volunteers to his purposes, not just conscripts to our own instincts. Humanity shares God's control of the planet and is made for fellowship with him. Indeed without God we lose our 'human-ness' and purpose-for-being altogether.

Two accounts of creation

The content of Genesis 1:
The creation of the world in seven days has been a problem to many. Here's one way of making sense of the passage that preserves the meaning without raising unnecessary problems.

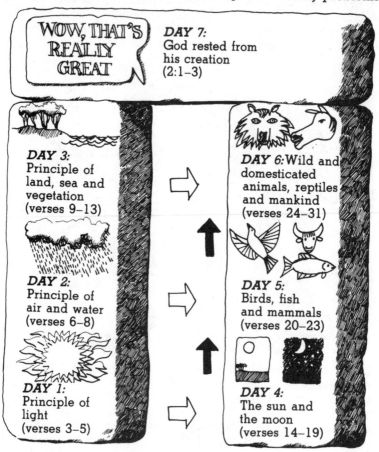

The teaching of Genesis 1:

☐ God is a God of order and reason, working systematically to a preconceived plan.
☐ God made the world out of nothing.
☐ The creation has a purpose behind it, each part fitting together to make a perfect whole.
☐ Mankind is the pinnacle of God's creation.

The content of Genesis 2:
In this complementary account of creation, two vivid metaphors are used to emphasize the dependence of humanity on its Creator.

We are *formed* by God as a potter fashions a vessel from clay. Man (*Adam*) was made from the ground (*adamah*).

HELLO ADAM

God *breathed* into us the breath of life. God animated us by his Spirit with loving intimacy.

Hi Eve baby

The teaching of Genesis 2:
- ☐ Man was made physically from the earth. We are not gods, but creatures fashioned out of common chemicals—like the birds, fish and animals.
- ☐ We may only be 'living dust', but we are 'walking miracles', brought into being by the self-giving act of God.

The God who is there

What message does God's handiwork have for us? Perhaps not a great deal about his character. For that we must go to his revelation in history (recorded in the Bible) and, in particular, in Jesus Christ.

But the creation does have something important to say. It tells us that the invisible God has given all people visible evidence of his 'eternal power and divine nature' (Romans 1:20). In other words the whole creation is shouting out to us 'He is there and he is God'.

He is there all right — behind the beautiful world that he has made. If people choose to ignore this, they have to do so willfully and stubbornly. He, not us, is God, the owner and controller of all things, the One on whom everything else, including us, should be centred.

The real tragedy

The fact that mankind turns its back on God does, of course, present us with a problem. If God is the Maker and Master of all things, the owner and controller of the universe, how come his top product does not, in general, accept this?

Unique among all the creatures, man is made in God's image, so reflecting in some way his very being and nature. But man is also God's rebel child, refusing his control, ignoring his love, living among his good and gracious gifts without even acknowledging him. What a mystery it all is. What a tragedy.

A spoiled universe

The Bible tells us that in some strange way our disobedience has affected the whole of creation. As its crown and pinnacle, our defection from God has done damage to the rest of what God has made — or at least held it back from reaching its full potential.

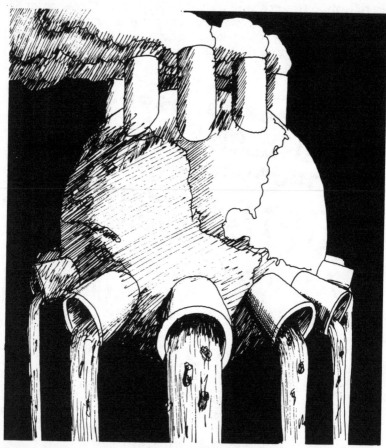

But the Bible also tells us that when God became part of his own creation, by being born into it in the person of Jesus, he set in motion a process of restoration. As man had been creation's downfall, so a man — Jesus — would be its Saviour. When God's redemptive power finally transforms those who trust in him, it will transform the whole creation as well.

So what?

If God created the world, what effect should this have on us?

1. It should give us a bigger view of God.

Knowing God's immense power and majesty should drive us to our knees in worship and prevent us from having small views about him. We should be permanently immunized against all illusions of grandeur or attempts to reduce God to human scale.

2. It should help keep us humble.

Not only is God great and mighty; he is also permanently related to us as Creator to created, Maker to made, Giver to receiver. We have nothing that he has not given us. We are nothing that he has not made. We are but thoughts in his mighty intellect.

3. It should make us more concerned about the environment.

We must tend and care for the environment, since God made it, loves it and has planned to transform it. Rather than adopting a cavalier or wasteful attitude, we should have a deeper appreciation of the created world — a desire to deal gently with it, protect it and preserve its wonderful creatures and resources.

4.

Conversion

How we come to know God personally

Changed people

People right down through the ages have encountered God in various ways — and have been changed. They have discovered Christianity as a revolutionary force that has turned their lives inside out.

Some classic testimonies from the past

St Augustine
(AD 354–430)
The greatest
theologian of the
Early Church and
a North African
bishop

After trying various philosophies, Augustine came under the preaching of Ambrose, Bishop of Milan. Augustine felt tied and bound by moral failure, especially in the area of his sexual life.

One day, in desperation, he rushed away from the company of friends into a quiet nook in a garden. He heard the voice of a child calling 'Take and read, take and read' and, opening the New Testament at the thirteenth chapter of Paul's letter to the Romans, he read: 'Let us conduct ourselves becomingly as in the day, not in revelling and drunkenness, not in debauchery and licentiousness, not in quarrelling and jealousy. But put on the Lord Jesus Christ and make no provision for the flesh, to gratify its desires.'

The dark clouds immediately lifted and the light of Christ broke upon him. He and his illegitimate son were baptized by Ambrose and he went on to become a prodigious writer, a profound theologian and later Bishop of Hippo.

John Wesley
(1703–1791)
Leader of the
English Revival
and founder
of Methodism

In the evening I went very unwillingly to a society in Aldersgate Street, where one was reading Luther's preface to the Epistle to the Romans. About a quarter before nine, while he was describing the change which God works in the heart through faith in Christ, I felt my heart strangely warmed. I felt I did trust in Christ, Christ alone, for salvation; and assurance was given me that he had taken away my sins, even mine, and saved me from the law of sin and death. [4]

Sir Wilfred Grenfell
(1865–1940)
Pioneer missionary to Labrador

It was so new to me that, when a tedious prayer-bore began with a long oration, I started to leave. Suddenly the leader, who afterwards I discovered was D. L. Moody, called out to the audience, 'Let us sing a hymn while our brother finishes his prayer.' His practicality interested me and I stayed the service out.

Later I went to hear the brothers J.E.K. and C.T. Studd speak at some subsidiary meeting of the Moody campaign. They were natural athletes and I felt I could listen to them. Never shall I forget that meeting of the Studd brothers, the audience being asked to stand up if they intended to try to follow Christ. It appeared a very sensible question to me, but I was amazed how hard I found it to stand up.

At last one boy out of a hundred or more, in sailor rig, suddenly arose. It seemed to me such a wonderfully courageous act, for I knew perfectly what it would mean to him, that I immediately found myself on my feet, and went out feeling that I had crossed the Rubicon and must do something to prove it. [5]

Sadhu Sundar Singh
(1889–1929?)
Indian saint and missionary to Tibet

[After rising to pray at 3.00 am] *I remained till about half-past-four praying and waiting and expecting to see Krishna or Buddha, or some avatar of the Hindu religion; they appeared not, but a light was shining in the room. I opened the door to see where it came from, but all was dark outside. I returned inside, and the light increased in intensity and took the form of a globe of light above the ground. In this light there appeared not the form I expected, but the living Christ, whom I had counted as dead.*

To all eternity I shall never forget his glorious and loving face, nor the words which he spoke: 'Why do you persecute me? See, I have died on the cross for you and for the whole world.' These words were burned into my heart as by lightning and I fell to the ground before him. My heart was filled with inexpressible joy and peace and my whole life was entirely changed. The old Sundar Singh died and a new Sundar Singh, to serve the living Christ, was born. [6]

C. S. Lewis
(1898–1963)
English academic and literary critic and Christian apologist

First stage (conversion to theism):
You must picture me alone in that room in Magdalen, night after night, feeling, whenever my mind lifted even for a second from my work, the steady unrelenting approach of him whom I so earnestly desired not to meet. That which I greatly feared had at last come upon me. In the Trinity term of 1929 I gave in, and admitted that God was God, and knelt and prayed:

Malcolm Muggeridge
(1903–)
English journalist, commentator and humorist

This is how I came to see my situation, in a sort of dream or vision, something more vivid and actual than most happenings and experiences. I am confined in the tiny dark dungeon of my ego, manacled with the appetites of the flesh, shackled with the inordinate demands of the will—a prisoner serving a life sentence with no hope of deliverance.

perhaps, that night, the most dejected and reluctant convert in all England. I did not see then what is now the most shining and obvious thing—the divine humility that will accept a convert even on such terms. The prodigal son at least walked home on his own feet. But who can duly adore that Love which will open the high gates to a prodigal who is brought in kicking, struggling, resentful and darting his eyes in every direction for a chance to escape? The words compelle intare, compel them to come in, have been so abused by wicked men that we shudder at them but, properly understood, they plumb the depth of divine mercy. The hardness of God is kinder than the softness of men, and his compulsion our liberation.

Second stage (during a trip to Whipsnade Zoo):
When we set out I did not believe that Jesus Christ is the Son of God and when we reached the zoo I did. Yet I had not exactly spent the journey in thought. Nor in great emotion. 'Emotional' is perhaps the last word we can apply to some of the most important events. It was more like when a man, after a long sleep, still lying motionless in bed, becomes aware that he is now awake. [7]

Then I notice high above me there is a window through which a faint glow of light comes filtering in—seemingly far away, remote and inaccessible; yet, I realize, a window looking out on to eternity. Inside, darkness, a place of fantasies and furies; outside, the white radiance of God's love shining through the universe—what the Apostle Paul called the glorious liberty of the children of God. And the window? I know what that is, too—the incarnation. Time and eternity intersecting in a cross. Now becoming always. God revealing himself as a man and reaching down to us, in order that we, reaching up, may relate ourselves to him.

Now I observe that the window is not, after all, far away, but near at hand, and that seen through it everything makes sense so that, like the blind man whose sight Jesus restored, I can say: 'One thing I know, that whereas I was blind, now I see.' Thenceforth, whenever I am looking through the window I see life as being full of joy and hope and brotherliness, whereas the moment I turn away the darkness encompasses me again. The ego once more lifts its cobra head, the servitude to the appetites and the will resumes. I am back in prison. Through the window I look out on reality; within, there is only fantasy. Oh the glory of reality, the horror of fantasy! The one, heaven; the other, hell—two states clearly differentiated as are light and darkness, joy and wretchedness, life and death. [8]

Charles Colson
(1931–)
Former personal adviser
to the US President
and convicted Watergate
criminal

In August of 1972, with the Watergate crisis about to explode on to the American public, Chuck Colson paid a private visit to Boston. There he met a Christian business executive, Tom Phillips. Phillips read to Colson an extract on pride from *Mere Christianity* by C. S. Lewis, which caught him unawares. Colson took the book away with him to read on a holiday in Maine.

I knew the time had come for me: I could not sidestep the central question Lewis (or God) had placed squarely before me. Was I to accept without reservations Jesus Christ as the Lord of my life? It was like a gate before me. There was no way to walk around it. I would step through, or I would remain outside . . . What I studied so intently all week opened a little wider the new world into which I had already taken my first halting, shaky steps. One week of study on the Maine coast would hardly qualify, even in the jet age, as much of an odyssey, but I felt as if I'd been on a journey of thousands of miles.

And so early that Friday morning, while I sat alone staring at the sea I love, words I had not been certain I could understand or say fell naturally from my lips: 'Lord Jesus, I believe in you. I accept you. Please come into my life. I commit it to you.'

With these few words that morning, while the briny sea churned, came a sureness of mind that matched the depth of feeling in my heart. There came something more: strength and serenity, a wonderful new assurance about life, a fresh perception of myself and the world around me. In the process, I felt old fears, tensions and animosities draining away. I was coming alive to things I'd never seen before, as if God was filling the barren void I'd known for so many months, filling it to its brim with a whole new kind of awareness. 9

Understanding conversion

'Repent and turn to God.'
'You must be born again.'
'You have been raised to life with Christ.'
'You are justified by faith.'
'Your sins are forgiven.'

These are some of the ways that the Bible uses to describe the experience of becoming a Christian. Each of these phrases tells of a big change occurring in our lives. Sometimes it is seen from God's side, i.e. by what he *does* in our personalities or the new status that he gives us. Sometimes it is seen from our side, i.e. by what we *receive* when we turn to God or the response that we make to God.

Why change?

We need to be changed because human beings are out of harmony with God. They are part of a rebel race and their hearts and minds are turned away from him. If they are to have any dealings with him at all, then somebody must change — and of course it cannot be God, who is entirely good and loving. It has to be us.

Because of his mercy and kindness, God himself makes the change possible. Through what his Son has done for us on the cross, we can be forgiven and brought into full fellowship with God. More than that, he puts into our minds in the first place the very idea that we should turn to him. Then he helps us make the necessary moral and spiritual revolution!

God, the people-changer

To put it simply, the big change is that we are converted from sin to God — there is a dramatic change of direction in our lives. Another way of saying this is that we turn from ourselves to God. Because of our rebellion against him — the Bible word for this is *sin* — we have become self-centred. So 'turning from sin' means 'turning from self'.

GO BACK

YOU ARE GOING THE WRONG WAY

Fortunately for us this does not mean the destruction of the self or the individual personality. God is not in the business of destroying people. Rather he changes the centre of people's lives — from the self-destructive egotism centred on self to the self-fulfilled ego centred on God. The Bible word for this is *repentance*, which literally means 'a change of mind', a complete about-turn in our attitude and actions regarding God, others and ourselves.

The crucial ingredient

Repentance's twin is faith. Faith replaces our old self-confidence with a whole-hearted trust in Jesus' death on the cross to win pardon and peace for us with God. Faith means deliberately accepting this and putting our whole confidence in it. And just as repentance turns us away from our old self-willed rebellion, so faith now commits us to a loving, trusting obedience to God. Faith is not just believing that the Christian faith is true: it is personally committing ourselves to the Christ about whom it speaks.

God does not accept us on the basis of what we have achieved — that's just a refined form of rebellion. Being what we are, we cannot help ourselves.

Rather God accepts us on the basis of what he has done for us through Christ.

Other religions

Do all roads lead to God?

'Religion' is notoriously hard to define. Just when we think we've worked out a satisfactory definition, some previously overlooked notion comes along to make it unworkable. For example, if we say religion is 'belief in a Supreme Being', then Buddhism is not concerned with such a belief. And what about Marxism? Is that a religion? Although it declares itself atheistic, Marxism often seems to behave like any other religion with its rituals and doctrines, saviour figures and holy places. What *is* religion?

The Bible does not define it. It accepts the fact that religions exist, but uses the term 'religion' sparingly and not always approvingly. In the Bible, our ideas about God are not important or, worse still, can get in the way of the real truth about him. The Bible speaks not of our search for God, but of his search for us. It tells us that he has come down into history to reveal himself and to rescue us from the self-destructive power of sin and guilt. And it tells us that this process came to a head in the coming of Jesus Christ—in his death and resurrection on our behalf.

Humanity is a strange mixture of good and evil, wisdom and folly, truth and falsehood. The religions of mankind reflect all of those things. Even the good that is in world religions can be used, because the human heart is so subtle and devious, to avoid coming in contact with the best, i.e. with God himself. 'If we have religion for our God,' someone has said, 'we will not have God for our religion.'

It is no use trying to combine all the religions. Each of them rejects that solution and, in any case, they are unmixable. To know God, we need to abandon our religious ideas (constructed to suit our own selfish ends) and open our hearts and minds to God himself. After all, he is the only One who knows the real truth about himself, a truth which often cuts right across our own dubious notions of him. As Jesus explained it to an intellectually honest but puzzled disciple: 'I am the way and the truth and the life. No man comes to the Father except by me.'

Comparative religion in a nutshell

❖❖

The Vedas said,
"Truth is one, but the sages speak
of it in many different ways."

The Buddha said,
"My teachings point the way
to attainment of the truth."

Mohammed said,
"The truth has been
revealed to me."

Jesus Christ says,

Jumping on the 'good works' bandwagon

Many people today resolutely assume that 'living a good life' will win them a way into heaven. But since this is done independently of God, it is actually the ultimate insult to him. Although it appears quite logical to trust one's self-effort, to do so denies the validity of Christ's death for us on the cross.

The divine resident

Conversion brings other benefits beside forgiveness. God promises that those who turn to him will be inwardly changed. They will be 'born anew' into a new kind of life, with new aims and perspectives — with new hopes, new inner resources and a new Jesus lifestyle.

The source of this quiet revolution is God's Spirit. He moves in with us as soon as we respond to his inward persuasion to turn to Christ. And he lives out in us the powerful new life that Jesus released into the world by defeating sin and death.

The Holy Spirit brings us into the whole new world and, as we learn to co-operate with him and rely on his power, we begin to be transformed into Jesus' likeness. Because we still belong to a rebel race and because sin has done us permanent damage, we will never (in this life) be perfect or completely Christ-like. But inwardly we have begun to be like him. Day by day we can become more and more Christ-like outwardly until finally, in heaven, we shall resemble him perfectly.

'When a man loves me, he follows my teaching. Then my father will love him, and we will come to that man and make our home within him.'

5.
Sanctification

How we become like Christ

Dark thoughts and smoke screens

Sometimes when people become Christians their joy is interrupted by a dark thought. The fact that they are forgiven and accepted by God is a source of great relief and happiness. But, and here is the anxiety, how can they be sure that in the days to come they will be able to actually *live* like Christians? God has, in a sense, prepared them for dying. But what about living?

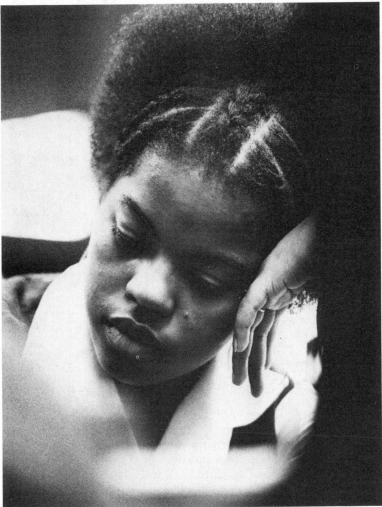

One of the most intriguing paradoxes of Christianity is that our efforts to live a good life can be both the biggest obstacle to our having a proper relationship with God and yet one of the clearest evidences that we do have one! Let us explain.

Human rebellion (sin) is turning from God and going it alone. Sometimes this results in immoral behaviour. But, often enough, it takes the form of respectability, high ideals, 'doing good' and even being quite religious. For God to break through to such people, they need to see their good behaviour may be just a 'smoke screen' for rebellion. They must, like Saul of Tarsus in the New Testament, abandon their confidence in their own goodness, apply for God's forgiveness and put on Christ's righteousness.

The goal of the Christian faith — not birth, but growth

It would be easy, then, for new Christians to think that behaviour was unimportant, perhaps still some kind of obstacle. But, and here is the paradox, once one has a true relationship with God, living a good life becomes very important. The difference is that it is no longer evidence of self-confident independence *from* God, but rather the result of a deep dependence *upon* him. God is, in fact, the source of the new life: he gives new motives, new directions and a new power to live by.

Once this great truth is understood, it helps remove the dark thoughts of failure that we mentioned earlier. The new Christian realizes that, although the Christian life is indeed beyond him, it is not beyond God. God is just as much involved in the rest of the Christian's life on earth as he has been in bringing him to faith in the first place. God not only brings spiritual babies into the world; he wants them to grow up. Like any good parent, he wants to raise healthy kids!

No more rules and regulations!

There are many guidelines in the New Testament. We have called them 'guidelines' rather than rules, because they are often more like principles than regulations. They have about them a certain freedom and flexibility which allow us to apply them to changing situations. True, God gave people laws in the beginning — like the Ten Commandments — and Jesus said that he did not come to abolish law, but to fulfil it. But it was in the fulfilling that a big change occurred.

As rebels against God, people had subconciously misunderstood the true purpose of his law. They had subtly misused it by turning it into a self-righteous way of life lived independently of God: they seemed to be living for him, but they were actually using the law against him, so as to shut him out of their lives. And so, when Jesus came to release us from our sins, he came also to release us from the law as used in this wrong way. He fulfilled it. He rescued it from misuse and put it where it belongs, i.e. not as a set of external rules, but as a principle inscribed on the Christian's heart — no longer a harsh legal constraint, but a new and willing attitude to please him and serve others. What a revolution!

The new law of Jesus

Do not think that I have come to do away with the Law of Moses and the teachings of the prophets. I have not come to do away with them, but to make their teachings come true.

YOU have heard that people were told in the past, 'Do not commit murder; anyone who does will be brought to trial.' But now I tell you: whoever is angry with his brother . . . will be in danger of going to the fire of hell.

YOU have heard that it was said, 'Do not commit adultery.' But now I tell you: anyone who looks at a woman and wants to possess her is guilty of committing adultery with her in his heart.'

*Y*OU have also heard that people were told in the past, 'Do not break your promise, but do what you have vowed to the Lord to do.' But now I tell you: do not use any vow when you make a promise.

*Y*OU have heard that it was said, 'An eye for an eye, and a tooth for a tooth.' But now I tell you: do not take revenge on someone who wrongs you. If anyone slaps you on the right cheek, let him slap your left cheek too.

*Y*OU have heard that it was said, 'Love your friends, hate your enemies.' But now I tell you: love your enemies and pray for those who persecute you . . . You must be perfect — just as your Father in heaven is perfect!

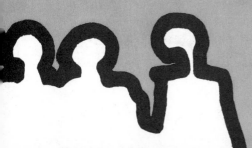

Partners with God

We have emphasized the point about keeping God's law because we think it is important. There is nothing that makes the Christian life so dull and dreary as turning it into a set of rules and regulations. And not only dull and dreary, but difficult — if not impossible — to live. It moves us back on to the old ground that Jesus came to save us from: from the deadly self-effort by which, in trying to go it alone, we effectively shut God out. The Christian life is to be a challenging and *exciting* partnership with God.

True, God has told us that there are things that we must do and things that we must avoid, but he has done so through these guidelines which help us adopt proper attitudes to life. And in this way he has lovingly allowed us as adult children to be part of the decision-making process. It certainly puts a whole new face on the business of living the Christian life.

Two tricky terms

People sometimes find words like 'holiness' or 'sanctification' rather off-putting. They are both technical terms — virtually the same word translated in different ways — to describe the moral and spiritual transformation that being a Christian involves. But these terms have been so badly misunderstood that they almost need reminting.

To many, sanctification suggests sanctimoniousness; holiness suggests an odd and isolated sort of life preoccupied with negative rather than positive things. Both words have overtones of superiority — of religious people looking disapprovingly down their long noses at struggling mortals like the rest of us. With such a poor mental image, who would want to be 'holy' or 'sanctified'?

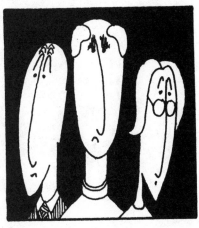

Three common misunderstandings of holiness:

You are a worm, an insignificant nothing in the eyes of God.

Having a negative self-image

Understanding sanctification

These words are one way of describing that partnership with God which is the essence of the Christian life. There are other ways of describing it, i.e. being recreated, being made new, being changed. And there are some helpful metaphors as well which illustrate the transformation from one angle or another.

Four metaphors for spiritual change:

Sanctification is, for example, like removing a grubby old set of clothes and putting on a new, clean set. Or like running hard from evil and dangerous things towards good and beautiful things. Or like a life and death struggle in which we kill off our old sinful desires, so that they may be replaced with motivations which come from God's Spirit. Or like the sowing of new Christian habits and thought-patterns, so that these will produce in us a new kind of Christ-like behaviour as its fruit.

Joining the family firm

From whichever way you look at it, the Christian life is a matter of partnership with God. Holiness is supremely the work of God's Spirit (he is specifically called the *Holy* Spirit nearly 100 times in the Bible). He is the power at work within the Christian. He gives us power to combat sin, power to be loyal and devoted to God, power to love and serve one another. Above all, he gives us the power to become more like Jesus in the rough and tumble of everyday life, especially when it comes to exhibiting that unique, sacrificial love that Jesus had for people.

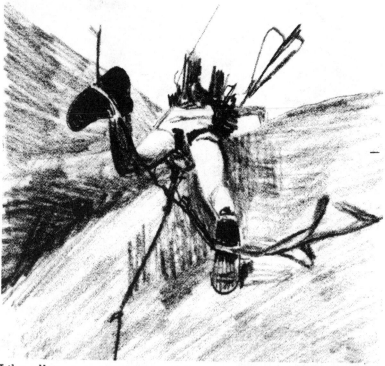

Like all true partnerships, this one invites our co-operation. For his part, God does not treat us as robots, doing things to us and in us without our willing co-operation. He inwardly prompts us, turning our minds towards the right way. But, for our part, we must by hundreds, thousands of choices and decisions allow him to go on forming in us a truly Christ-like character.

It is, from one angle, a hard and costly business, a constant life-long self-discipline in the fierce battle against sin and selfishness. But on the other hand it is really possible, because the Senior Partner is constantly at work within us. In all the New Testament there is no verse which puts it more clearly than this:

Keep on working with fear and trembling to complete your salvation, because God is always at work in you to make you willing and able to obey his own purpose (Philippians 2:13).

So he is at work. We are at work. It is a partnership.

SENIOR PARTNER

OGILVIE
&
OGILVIE

Truly holy, truly human

When we really understand how sanctification works, it removes any negative misunderstanding. Far from making us into odd and isolated people, it actually makes us more normal and related to life. As Jesus said, we are in the world but not of it, i.e. we are not to be controlled by its false and selfish values and God-denying ways, but we are, as he was, committed to identifying ourselves with needy people.

There is a negative side to this: we must, with God's help, separate ourselves from all those things which spiritually hurt and destroy us. But the positives of the Christian life far outweigh the negatives. Committing ourselves wholeheartedly to God is the best antidote there is against falling under the power of evil.

Holiness is actually more 'normal' than unholiness, because it has a truly humanizing effect. It renews us, says Paul, in the image of our Creator. And bearing his image is, after all, what God originally created humans for.

What's more when God became man, he gave us a very vivid model of what true humanity looks like. God has done this not by setting us a high and unattainable example to follow, but by sending us his Spirit to live within us. As Jesus lived a fully human life, overcoming humanity's twin destroyers of sin and death, so the Spirit helps us reproduce all over again that peerless life in our own daily situations. By making us one with his Son and adopting us into his own family, God now makes it possible for us to show, in a desperately needy world, the family likeness of heaven. And this Jesus-life is thoroughly natural and human.

The balanced life

A key metaphor for sanctification is that of *growing*. The apostle Paul defines this more clearly by describing it from nine different angles: 'the fruit of the Spirit is love, joy, peace, patience, kindness, goodness, faithfulness, gentleness, self-control' (Galatians 5:22 and 23). These characteristics can be described as three types of relationships:

1. With God:
love
joy
peace

2. With others:
patience
kindness
goodness

3. With ourselves:
faithfulness
gentleness
self-control

All this beautiful fruit is the one work of the one Spirit. It is not God's intention that we should 'specialize' by being strong on one, weak on others. He wants us to have a complete, all-round set of balanced relationships.

But the New Testament summarizes all our obligations in one of these characteristics: *love.* It is the greatest of all virtues, the one word that sums up all obligations, the one quality which will endure beyond the end of time. With Jesus as our model, it should not surprise us that his own loving attitudes and actions should be the most characteristic part of our family likeness.

Citizens of two worlds

How can we be citizens of heaven, while solidly based in this world? On one hand the New Testament gives us a glowing picture of the Christian. He is a new person, dead to sin and alive to God, a 'saint' seated with Christ on God's throne. Paul sometimes writes as if we are in heaven already!

But there is a grimmer side to life. We often feel earthbound and unspiritual, defeated and almost unChristian in our attitudes and actions. The New Testament endorses this. It reminds us that, while forgiven, we still bear the marks of human rebelliousness. So we are warned to take sin seriously, to flee temptation and to come often to God for cleansing from sin.

How can these two apparently contradictory elements be reconciled? The New Testament simply tells us that we live in two worlds. In Christ we have stepped into a whole new order in which the blessings of the future — being declared 'not guilty' by God, possessing eternal life, being indwelt by God's own Spirit — are all ours now.

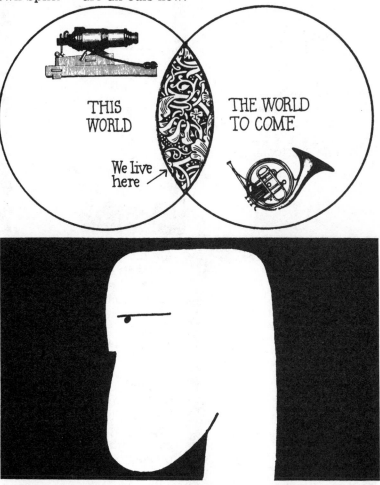

But this does not mean that we are entirely free from the older order, damaged as it is by sin. We still have strong links with it. The 'world, the flesh and the devil' still exert tremendous pressure and will do so to the end. We must live out our lives in the tension between these two realities.

Detours and dead-ends

If we concentrate only on the positive things that are said about the Christian in the New Testament, we will drift into 'perfectionism', i.e. we will be so programmed for *success* that we will take sin too lightly, underestimating its steady and subtle power. We will be tempted to 'sanctify' all that we do, whether it is from God or not, excusing or explaining away our inevitable shortcomings.

On the other hand, if we concentrate only on the negative side, we will be so programmed for *failure* that we will play down God's victory through Christ and adopt a rather gloomy approach to the Christian life. We will think that it is so much God's work that we'll minimize our role in the partnership. We must avoid both extremes — being either too presumptuous (thinking we are near perfect) or too pessimistic (feeling we are spiritually inferior).

Reaching for the summit

A clear picture of our life in two worlds is the only way to keep our spiritual sanity. In practice this should lead to the following:

1. Being honest and open:

We must not be preoccupied with sin and failure, but we must be honest and realistic about it just the same. We must go on facing up to our sins and confessing them to God, trusting him to forgive us and wipe the slate clean. We must accept from God the great gift of repentance, asking him to deliver us from those things of which we are ashamed and co-operating with him as he does so.

2. Being obedient:

We have turned from self to Jesus. He is our new Lord and we must seek to obey his every wish and command. We must constantly offer our ordinary everyday selves (our bodies) to him so that all we have and all we are can be used in his service. In doing this, we'll find those Christian guidelines considered earlier so essential.

3. Co-operating with God's Spirit:

As we have seen, the Spirit is the secret force in Christian living. So we must be sensitive to him, obedient to his promptings and leadings, avoiding at all costs those things which offend him and silence his voice.

This does not, of course, cancel out our need to put every personal effort into living the Christian life. Remember, it is a partnership, a co-operative venture so close and united that there is no dividing between his part and ours.

4. Going to heaven:

This may surprise you, but the Christian life and our sanctification will always be incomplete in this world. We will never reach perfection till we are face-to-face with God. Our present likeness to Jesus is real enough, but it is inward and often veiled by failure. Jesus too is 'hidden', not yet acknowledged as humanity's true and rightful king.

But Jesus will 'appear' in glorious triumph and, when that day dawns, the old hindrances and obstacles to seeing him will disappear. We will appear with him as totally transformed, Spirit-controlled, Christ-like people.

That's really something to get excited about . . . and look forward to.

6.
Church

Why we meet with our fellow Christians

Individual, but not individualistic

Becoming a Christian is a very personal thing. No one can do it for you. You cannot inherit it from your parents. You cannot 'catch' it by joining a church, or have it passed on to you mechanically in a religious ceremony. No, you must personally choose Christ and turn to him as if you were the only person who had ever done so. It is an individual decision.

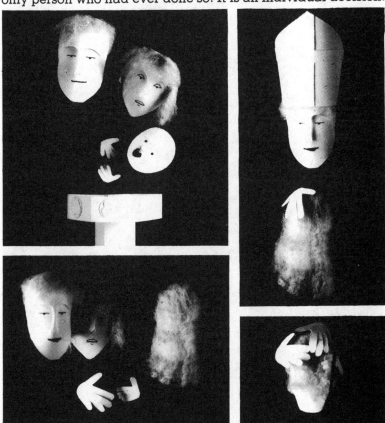

But, because it is so individual, we must not assume that the Christian life is a life of individualism. Rather the reverse. From the moment that we belong to Christ we belong to all others who belong to him as well. If we are to make progress in the Christian life, we cannot possibly do so by going it alone. And it is at this point that the church, rightly understood, becomes very important to us.

Stereotypes and other mental blocks

The church, however, is often not rightly understood. To many it is an institution — and a stuffy and stodgy one at that. Or else it is a building, dark and gloomy inside, where dreary incomprehensible rituals are performed with very little relevance to everyday life. Or it is 'the clergy', that hierarchy of moralizers who are mostly out of touch, and whose main aim in life seems to be fostering dull respectability and preventing people from enjoying themselves.

These ideas are, of course, part of a mental stereotype often held by people not actually connected with a real, live, local church. The fact is that some churches and churchmen are sometimes like these negative mental images. But others are not remotely like this at all. To go on thinking so may be little more than a convenient way of avoiding the personal challenge found in an actual local church. In any case, what the New Testament means by 'church' is much more important than any mental picture we might have of it or any of our poor, fumbling attempts to be a church in any given locality.

Defining 'church'

The word translated 'church' in the New Testament is the Greek word *ekklesia*. It is a general term for *a meeting* or an assembly, and was used in secular Greek to describe gatherings of free citizens who had come together to discuss and decide upon important civil matters.

But from Old Testament times the word had also been used to describe a meeting *called by God*. It was a get-together which he had arranged for his own purposes and to which he had called people to come.

In the New Testament *ekklesia* is really only used after the resurrection of Jesus. It is a post-resurrection get-together, called partly to witness to the world that Jesus has risen from the dead and established God's glorious new order. Because Jesus has given his own Spirit to this remarkable new assembly, any meeting of Christians is really a foretaste of the final gathering which will take place at the end of history.

We meet today to commemorate the death and resurrection of Jesus. We look forward to the time when he will come again.

And yet, since the church is made up of fallible human beings, it is still very much part of this world, often opposed, persecuted and tempted. Its heart may be in heaven, but its feet are firmly planted on the ground. Or, to change the metaphor, it is like a clay pot containing spiritual treasure. It is only as we keep both these dimensions firmly fixed in our minds that we will understand the true stature of the church and, at the same time, cope with its faults and failings.

The heavenly invitation

If God has called this meeting we call the church, why has he done so? Apart from the fact that it is a sign to the world (and even to supernatural powers) that his kingdom has been established, the church has a big part to play in the spiritual growth of each and every one of its members. In fact the church is so essential to their growth that they cannot really get along without it. Those who try soon fall by the wayside.

We were made for each other. When God created us, he made us for community.

The saga of Steve Solitary:

The real-life possibility

No one can become a whole person without relationships with others. Tiny babies die for lack of it. Growing children can be emotionally crippled without enough of it. Adult human beings find or lose themselves on the grounds of their relationships with others.

If this is true of us as God's creation, it is doubly true of us as his new creation in Christ Jesus. We need each other. We need to serve and be served by each other. We can only grow as individuals when we surrender our individualism so as spiritually to build each other up and to build up the whole community, the church, to which we all belong. It is so important for us to grasp this paradoxical truth: that we can only really become ourselves in Christ when we cease to be so preoccupied with self and begin to invest our lives in our fellow believers.

A close-up of a caring community:

A life that matters

Investing one's life in others was, after all, the pattern Jesus followed. He did not come, he said, to be served, but to serve and to give his life sacrificially for others. He did this daily in his relationships with his friends and with the crowds that he ministered to; finally he did it to the limit on the cross. And he taught his disciples in many challenging ways that this was the path that they too must follow.

On one occasion he washed their dirty feet. On another occasion he placed a child in their midst and reminded them that the greatest among them should be the youngest and the leader the one who serves. In this he gave us an unforgettable pattern for the way in which we must serve each other.

The word 'service' or 'ministry' in the New Testament covers anything and everything that any Christian is able to do for God or for others. It originally described the work of a table-waiter, but eventually became a general term for service. In the church it is applied to mundane practical tasks just as much as to the more spectacular spiritual ministries like preaching, teaching or leading. The person who cleans out the church building is just as much 'in the ministry' as the noted Bible teacher who is billed to preach next Sunday. Nor does our service have to be 'churchy': service for Christ and for others is often best done in the homes, offices, factories and classrooms of those who need our help.

My wife Louise and I just l-e-r-v being in your beautiful country.

SPECIAL INTERNATIONAL GUEST PREACHER

The Rev. Dr. Larry Loquacious

TOPIC:

The Eschatological Significance of the Last Times in the Isaianic Texts in Matthew's Gospel

I JUST L-E-R-V DOWN-TO-EARTH PREACHING

God's management chart

*S*O *he who came down is the same one who went up, above and beyond the heavens, to fill the whole universe with his presence.*

It was he who 'gave gifts to men': he appointed some to be apostles, others to be prophets, others to be evangelists, others to be pastors and teachers. He did this to prepare all God's people for the work of Christian service, to build up the body of Christ. And so we shall all come together to that oneness in our faith and in our knowledge of the Son of God: we shall become mature men, reaching to the very height of Christ's full stature.

EPHESIANS 4:10-13 (GNB)

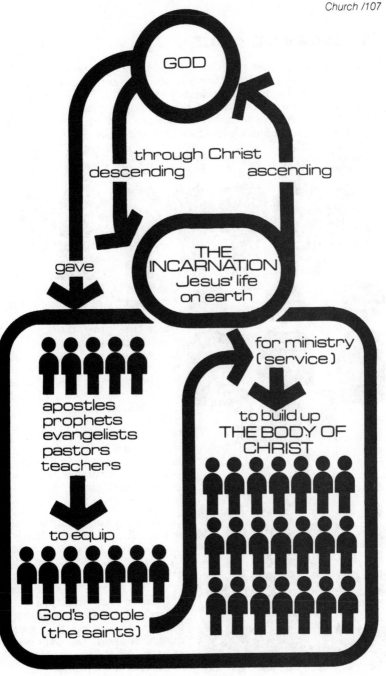

Ministers and ministry

By calling all Christians 'ministers', we are not suggesting that the work of preaching and pastoring is unimportant. These specialist tasks need to be put in a right perspective. They are vitally important for the simple reason that God uses them to equip all Christians for their own unique individual ministries. Pastors and teachers are in the church to minister to ministers!

Church members are mainly equipped by being taught the word of God. It is the food by which they grow, the nourisment by which they become wise and mature, and the means by which they in turn become teachers of others. New Christians start with 'milk' — the simple basic truths — and then go on to 'solids' as they are able to cope with them. Through this process they are enabled to find out what their particular ministry in the church should be and how to exercise it.

To be effectively equipped is not a matter of merely sitting and listening to sermons: new Christians must be motivated and activated for service. And to do this a more intimate kind of training is necessary, a 'learning laboratory' in which they are able to ask their own questions and to discover how to apply what they are taught to their everyday lives.

The three faces of the live community

The church looks in three directions. As we have seen, it looks *inwards* to loving and sacrificial service between its members. However, if it does only that, it will soon become inbred and static. It must also look *outwards* to a world adrift from God and alienated from his presence.

Together with the inward and outward look, the church must also look *upwards* to God. It is a meeting, an assembly, a get-together which he has called. Those who have responded to his call must therefore look to him as their heavenly Chairman and President. What does he want? What is his will? They must listen to him, talk to him, focus upon his glory and grace, praise and adore him. In short, they must worship him.

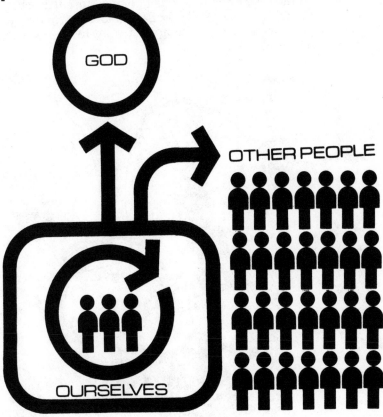

Giving God his due

The old Anglo-Saxon *weorthscipe* means to attribute worth to someone or something, to give 'worthship' or due. 'The chief end of man', says one great catechism, 'is to glorify God and enjoy him forever'. For this we were made. From this we turned away. But as God redeems us in Christ, he awakens again in our hearts the capacity to look again upon his beauty and his majesty and make what response we can.

What a joy it will be some day to do it in his presence, freed finally from everything that obscures his glory. What joy it already is, as we turn from self to acknowledge his greatness and power and declare our constant total dependence upon him for all things. The Psalmists of the Old Testament nearly burst their voice-boxes as they rejoiced in God and shouted his praises to the sky. They teach us to leave our earthbound ways and fly with them to his footstool, to fling ourselves before him and praise him for being just what he is — great, good and beautiful.

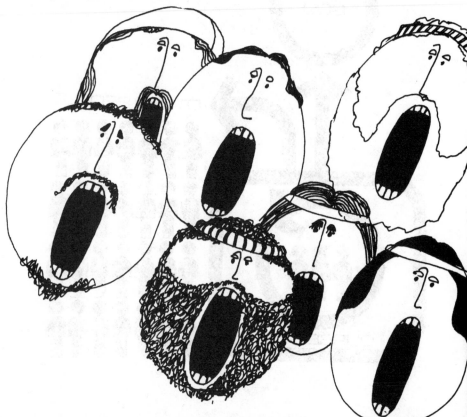

WORSHIP is the submission of all our nature to God. It is the quickening of the conscience by his holiness, the nourishment of the mind with his truth, the purifying of the imagination by his beauty, the opening of the heart to his love, the surrender of the will to his purpose — and all this gathered up in adoration, the most selfless emotion of which nature is capable and therefore the chief remedy for that self-centredness which is our original sin and the source of all actual sin.[10]

ARCHBISHOP WILLIAM TEMPLE

I HAD never noticed that all
enjoyment spontaneously
overflows into praise unless
(sometimes even if) shyness or the
fear of boring others is deliberately
brought in to check it. The world
rings with praise: lovers praising
their mistresses, readers their
favourite poet, walkers praising the
countryside, players praising their
favourite game — praise of weather,
wines, dishes, actors, motors,
horses, colleges, countries, historical
personages, children, flowers,
mountains, rare stamps, rare
beetles, even sometimes politicians
and scholars.

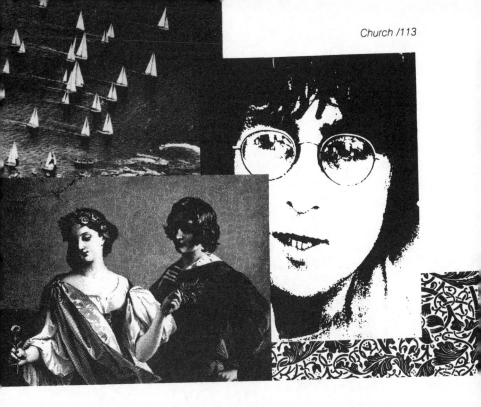

I had not noticed how the humblest
and, at the same time, most
balanced and capacious minds
praised most . . . I had not noticed
either that, just as men
spontaneously praise whatever they
value, so they spontaneously urge us
to join them in praising it: 'Isn't she
lovely?' 'Wasn't it glorious?' 'Don't
you think that magnificent?' The
psalmists, in telling everyone to
praise God, are doing what all men
do when they speak of what they
care about.[11]

C.S. LEWIS

Worship: secular and sacred

Of course worship is not limited to what we do in church. When we offer our whole selves to the Lord on the altar of daily living, our homes and workplaces become a shrine, mundane tasks a holy and acceptable sacrifice. God is not so pious as to exclude from worship our everyday lives and practical tasks. He makes no false distinction between 'sacred' and 'secular' — and neither should we.

IF THIS IS WORSHIP, WHY DOESN'T HE ENJOY IT MORE?

Having said that, let us emphasize that the particular kind of worship offered to God in the church, i.e. as the special company of people that he has called together, is important both to him and to us. There, forgetful of self and loving each other, we lift up our hearts and voices as best we know how to give him his due. Our weak fumbling attempts to do justice to his majesty are a sacrifice he gladly accepts and delights in. Our cracked and broken strains are music to his ears.

Growth: quality and quantity

The church looks upwards to God; it looks inward to its own fellowship. But it will soon become little more than a sterile religious club if it does not also look outward to a needy world. In fact its growth must have two dimensions: quality and quantity.

If the maturity of its members increases at the expense of a lack of concern for non-members, it will soon become introverted and lose its maturity. If it merely adds new people to itself without depending on the quality of their lives, it will soon become shallow and lose its clear-cut Christian shape. If this tendency becomes too pronounced, it will probably also begin to lose its numbers as well. A proper balance between growth in quality and quantity is essential.

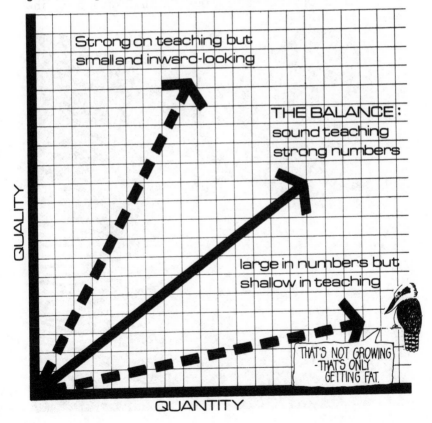

A people movement

When it comes to reaching people with the Christian message, some are more gifted than others. But the whole church — the body of Christ — needs to see itself as part of the action. If those who win others are the lips or tongue of the body, then its legs must also be used to take them to where the message needs to be delivered, its ears must tune in to the expressed needs of those being evangelized, its hands must serve them and so give credibility to the loving power of the message.

The whole body expresses and exemplifies the gospel. If people respond to it, then the whole body, especially those who are particularly gifted in this direction, will be needed to nourish and nurture them. From the beginning to the end the local church is essential to the spiritual growth of the individual Christian.

7.
Prayer

Why and how we talk to God

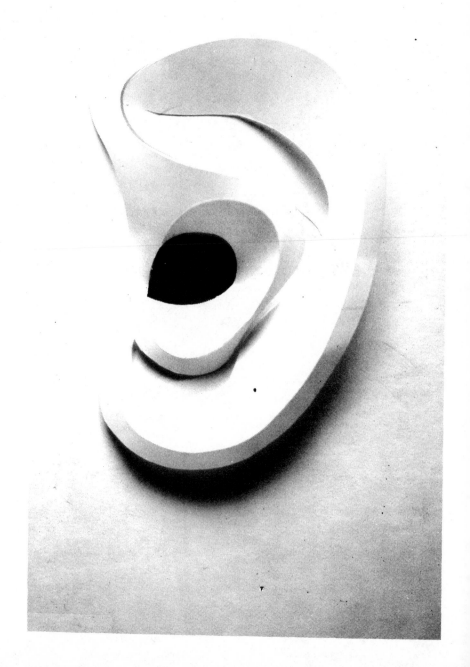

Prayer: a conversation between friends

Prayer is talking to God. It is also listening to God. In other words, prayer is communication between God and ourselves. And since Christianity is the story of how God has made friends with us, his formerly hostile creatures, such communication is obviously very important. It is hard to imagine a friendship without communication or conversation between the friends. And it is equally hard to imagine a person claiming to know God, but not praying.

The heart of the problem

'I don't need to pray'

Prayer is one of those activities more talked about than done. Unless it is the purely mechanical kind, like the pagan turning a prayer wheel or the nominal Christian mumbling a set formula, prayer is a challenge to our independence and thus often avoided.

Alienated from God, we find it hard to admit we need him. Although God has reconciled us through Christ, we still have to do battle with our independent, go-it-alone attitude. There is part of us which would rather cope with life unaided, which prefers to confer with itself rather than commune with God. For this we need forgiveness and help.

We need to overcome this preoccupation with self and be brought back to where we truly belong: in a creature-Creator relationship with God. That means total dependence and total dependence involves prayer.

'I don't feel like praying'

The way to learn about prayer is to pray! If we have a relation-ship with God then, as one praying Christian from the past used to say, we must 'learn to do ourselves violence in the matter of prayer'. In other words we must get tough with our-selves. We shall find that many of the problems we have with prayer are solved by the act of praying.

In one sense launching into prayer when you don't feel like it is a venture of faith. It is also an act of self-discipline, part of the daily 'crucifixion' of the self that leads to a 'resurrection' to better things. And the joy of fellowship with God is one of these benefits. This joy soon takes over and dissolves our former unwillingness — as indeed do the answers to prayer that we experience. Like many things in the Christian life, it is the *beginnings* that are the battleground. Once we are involved in these activities, they become such a reality to us that our hesitations and fears disappear. This is certainly the case with prayer.

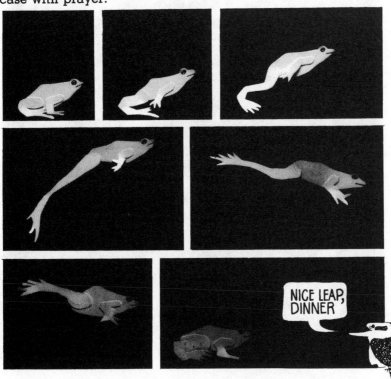

Models of prayer

The most profound teaching on prayer in the New Testament comes from Jesus himself. He was, of course, born into a praying people. At every stage in the Old Testament we find people praying. Apart from the examples of great men of prayer like Abraham, Moses, Daniel and Jeremiah, at least eighty-five original prayers have been counted in the Old Testament, together with sixty whole psalms and fourteen parts of psalms which could be called prayers.

Jesus himself prayed often: with his disciples, in secret, in times of spiritual conflict and crisis, when he was on the cross. He gave thanks to God; he sought guidance from him and communed with him; he interceded for others. In and through it all he addressed God as 'Father' and encouraged us to do the same, i.e. to see God as caring more for us and more anxious to talk with us than any earthly parent.

A matter of right attitudes

God is not supersensitive when we are honest with him. He is not touchy or easily offended when we speak frankly to him about our problems. Indeed, Jesus positively encouraged his followers to share openly with God *all* their concerns. He wants us to do the same today.

Much of Jesus' teaching on prayer is found in the parables. There Jesus identified four characteristics his disciples were to have when they prayed.

1. He commended tenacity in prayer

For example, there is the story of the persistent man who wakes his friend at midnight and will not stop asking for the help he so badly needs.
Or again, there is the story of the tenacious woman who gives a careless judge no rest until he settles her case.

2. He commended compassion in prayer

There is the story of the unjust servant who, although released from his debt for a large sum of money, sued one of his debtors for a much smaller sum, thus refusing to pass on to another the kind of practical consideration he had himself received.

3. He commended humility in prayer

There is the story of the
religious leader, proud of his
social exclusiveness and moral
superiority, and the tax
racketeer who was filled with a
sense of remorse at his own
unworthiness. God ignored the
prayers of the first and
honoured those of the second.

4. He commended faith in prayer

There is the story of faith as
small as the smallest grain that
can command a hill to 'move
over there!' and it does — a
sign of unseen faith at work in
a spectacular way.

In all this, Jesus' teaching on prayer comes through loud and
clear. We may, he is saying, persistently bring our requests to
a generous God. We do so not because God is unwilling to
help, but because he wishes to develop and deepen our faith.
We must pray for others with a compassionate heart, not just
to follow Christ's example, but to prove we are truly forgiven.
We must come to God humbly, conscious of our smallness and
sinfulness, but confident of his love and forgiveness.

We should come to God boldly, with a sane estimate of our
own limitations, but with an expectant trust in God's ability to
bring about change: in ourselves, others, our local church, our
workplace — even in society at large.

The model prayer

When Jesus' disciples asked him to teach them to pray, he gave them the Lord's Prayer. This prayer is not to be used just as a set prayer for constant repetition. It is useful for that and is often employed in church services in this way. But, more specifically, it is a *pattern prayer*. It sets out things that need to be prayed for and puts them in the right order of priority as well.

God's work

In the Lord's Prayer there are six petitions. The first three concern God and his affairs. This is the right order for prayer: God first and then us.

We ask that *God's name be 'hallowed'*, i.e. that God's honour and glory be acknowledged and accepted. We ask that *his kingdom come*, i.e. that God's control of the world and its history be brought right out into the open and that he remove all that opposes him. We ask that *his will be done on earth as in heaven*, i.e. that people will come to accept God's rightful control of their lives and that they will anticipate now the life of his coming kingdom, the very life of heaven itself in which he is worshipped and obeyed.

Our needs

The next three petition in the Lord's Prayer deal with us and our needs. We ask that *God will give 'bread' to us day by day*, i.e. that he will meet all our practical needs (though not necessarily all our 'wants'). We ask God to *forgive us our sins* — a request as urgent and as constantly needful as for our daily bread. And we discover, in making this request, that the spirit in which forgiveness is received is identical with the one that forgives others. If we cannot pass forgiveness on to others, then this is positive proof that we haven't got the right attitude to receive forgiveness from God.

The last request is that *God leads us not into temptation*, i.e. that he will not allow us to be put to the test. God, for our education and growth, does test us in the same way as our earthly examiners do. But the Christian soon learns how weak and vulnerable he or she is and so we avoid trying ourselves out against temptation. Rather we approach temptation with a sense of divine realism, knowing that we are completely in God's hands, but not lowering our guard. It is the only safe way.

Our Father who art
in heaven,
Hallowed be thy name.
Thy kingdom come.
Thy will be done
on earth
as it is in heaven.
Give us this day
our daily bread;
And forgive us our debts,
As we also have forgiven
our debtors;
And lead us not into
temptation,
But deliver us from
evil.

In Jesus' name

Jesus taught us to offer prayer 'in his name'. Because he has won access to God's presence for us on the cross, we can now approach God with real confidence. Jesus' 'name' also means that we must pray in the same way as he did, i.e. that God's will should be done in our lives and in the lives of others.

If all this seems a tall order we should remember that, like every other aspect of the Christian life, we are not on our own. God's Spirit, the Spirit of Christ himself, is 'inside' us praying as well. Even if we are not sure what needs to be prayed about, we can be sure that the Spirit knows. It is really God praying *to* God *through* us!

A five-point pattern

You may find that a pattern of prayer like the following is helpful:

1. Look up: adoration

Look first to God and express your appreciation for who and what he is. It may well be that some passages from the Bible, perhaps the Psalms, will help you express your adoration.

2. Look in: confession

Looking at God often throws our own lives into stark relief. There is much to be ashamed of — much to repent of and confess. But as we bring our sins to God, we have the great assurance of forgiveness because of what Jesus has done for us on the cross. It is, therefore, not morbid introspection that we engage in, but realistic self-examination.

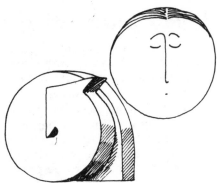

3. Look around: intercession

This is prayer for others, prayer 'with names in it'. And there is no greater service that we can do our friends and neighbours than bear them up to God in prayer. Some people find a notebook of names for each day a real help in intercession.

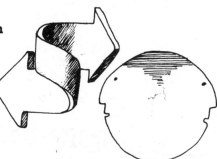

4. Look back: thanksgiving

All that we have and all that we are comes from God. How easy it is to take it for granted. Let us be more concerned 'to give credit where credit is due' by thanking God from the heart for all his goodness and loving kindness to us day by day.

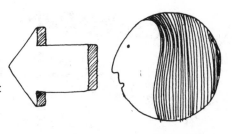

5. Look forward: petition

We have many needs for body and soul. Let us bring them before God, the generous Giver. As someone has put it so well:

*You are coming to a King,
Large petitions with you bring.*

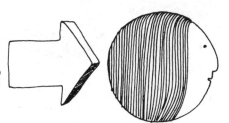

Some practical pointers

There are many books on prayer and many practical suggestions about how to pray. To pray effectively implies we are properly organized. Here are some useful tips:

(a) *Make time to pray,* since prayer will not make time for itself. It is all very well to say that our whole life is one of worship and that we can pray anywhere at any time, but human beings are not built that way. They need to have special times for concentrating on prayer if they want the rest of their lives to be prayerful. Having no special time soon means that no time is special.

(b) *Spend time in prayer,* turning off the everyday, turning over our thoughts to God and tuning in to the word and presence of God.

It is no good excusing a patchy prayer-life on the grounds that 'it is the quality not quantity that matters'. A husband may be able to give his wife a peck at the door as he grabs his briefcase on his way to work, but that had better not be the extent of his communication with her. In the same way God wants more than a morning grunt as we clean our teeth, or even a friendly wave at the gate.

(c) *Cultivate the art of listening to God,* practising the ancient biblical art of meditation and establishing our spiritual roots deep into God. Just as it takes years for a husband and wife to develop the close bonds of affection, so our relationship with God can only develop by spending time with him over a period of time.

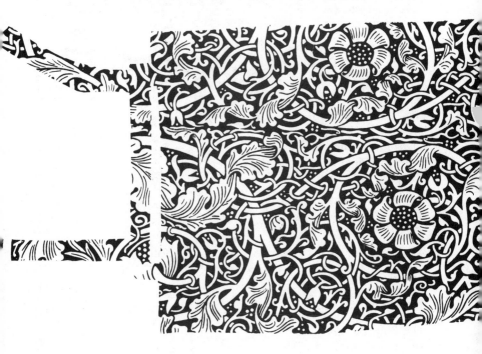

Making it work

Three last words of advice:

1. Take the Bible into your prayers

Let God start the
conversation and do
not change the
subject! The Bible
checks, challenges,
accuses, encourages
and strengthens us.
It will soon give us
plenty to praise,
thank and ask God for.

2. Take the day into your prayers

Each day you have
things to do, people
to cope with, new
problems to face.
You have your
hopes, dreams and
desires. All of these
can be brought to
God in prayer.

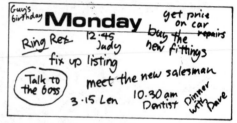

3. Take yourself into your prayers

You are an important
person in your own
right — someone for
whom Christ died.
God has his own
hopes and plans for
your life. In your
prayers, seek his will
for you and bring
yourself into line
with it. Surrender all
that you have and
all that you are to
him. Pray that you
and God together
will find the very
best there is in life
for you.

But remember, the best way to learn about praying is to pray!

8.
Judgement

How wrongs will be put right

Four common misconceptions

People today often view God in one of four ways:

(a) As a grim, foreboding authority figure, 'down' on simple human pleasures

(b) As a peaceful but vague 'force', useful in an emergency

(c) As a benign but distant being whom we never bother — and hope he doesn't bother us

(d) As a kindly grandfather figure, who is good for handouts and is ever tolerant of human failings.

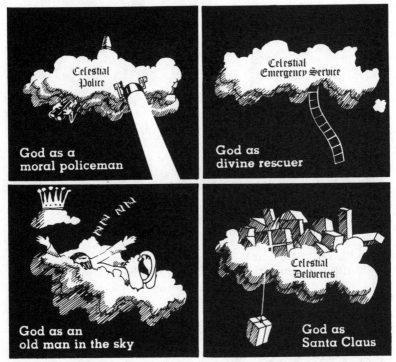

God as a
moral policeman

God as
divine rescuer

God as an
old man in the sky

God as
Santa Claus

Each of these views contains an element of truth. God *is* concerned with how people behave and the quality of relationships between them. God *is* vitally interested in meeting people at their point of need and listens when they call to him. He *is* a transcendent God, who stands above and beyond his creation. He *is* a generous Father, who enjoys sharing gifts with his children and is willing to forgive.

But on their own these four views are at best half-truths that prevent us seeing the full truth about God. How are we to understand God's character?

The flip side of love

If people believe in God at all, they probably mostly think about him as a God of love. This is correct. Love is, as some Christians in the past used to say, his 'proper' work. It is his nature — God *is* love — and so, together with similar activities like being kind, showing mercy and forgiving, love is most natural to him.

God saved you because he loves you and wants you to be his people.

But God's love is not of the wishy-washy, anything-goes kind. It is too pure and passionate for that, and it burns with fierce indignation against all that spoils or detracts from the character of those he loves. He values us too much to water down the high standards that he has for us. In any case, he knows that it is no good sweeping under the carpet our rebellious attitudes and actions. They must come out into the open and be acknowledged. They must be judged and dealt with. Then, and only then, is it possible for us to be reconciled to him on a true and loving basis.

If you don't obey his law, he will judge you. Our God is a holy God.

A love with demands

So love and judgement can and must go together. And they do right throughout the Bible, particularly when it climaxes in the life, death and resurrection of Jesus. Jesus lived and preached love. He showed how far God's affection extended to people, even to the moral outcasts and riff-raff of the day. He constantly taught that God is our loving and compassionate Father.

But Jesus also exposed sin, and not just in the externals either. He uncovered the unseen thoughts and intentions of the heart, warning that even hidden things would be brought out into the light of God's judgement

A love that paid the price

When Jesus went to the cross, love and judgement were plainly and clearly revealed. Judgement fell upon him from heaven and exacted the supreme penalty for sins past, present and future — for our sins of thought, word and deed. But it was love that took him to the cross and bound him there, love that met and paid all our debts. No sin was overlooked, no shortcoming brushed aside, no justice left undone for, as we have seen, this is how God in all his holy and gracious realism loves.

God is not sentimental about sin. He searches it out and uncovers it: he identifies it, accuses it and brings it into the dock. But, when he does so, it is his own great heart of love that meets all the penalties and opens to us a doorway into a new and living relationship with him. This is judgement indeed. This is love indeed.

People today do not always hold love and judgement together so easily, probably because the standpoint from which they view them is not always that of Jesus' cross. Many find it very easy to believe in a God of love, but very hard to believe in a God of judgement — and almost impossible to reconcile the two. In such an atmosphere even Christians stop talking about God's judgement and start getting hazy ideas about the fate of rebellious mankind. A God of love, they think, will not take too strong a line with us. He will accept us all in the end — good, bad and indifferent. In any case, too much concentration on judgement by preachers will frighten away potential converts and fill their heads with unhealthy fears and feelings of guilt.

Taking judgement seriously

We are not suggesting that our message be filled with gloom and doom, or that we go out of our way to frighten people into the kingdom of God. But if the Bible stresses the theme of judgement so strongly, and this is not incompatible with God's love but the *other side* of it, then it is up to us to take the concept of God's judgement very seriously.

Indeed we owe it to people, not just because the Bible says so — a good enough reason in itself — but because we must not allow people to be the victims of an evil conspiracy. If humanity has highjacked Planet Earth and tried to blackmail God, then there can be no shadow of doubt that this stupid and immoral rebellion will be put down. We must warn people that this is so, but in doing so also tell them the joyous news that the planet's owner and rightful ruler has provided a free and generous amnesty for them.

The Long Silence

*A*T the end of time, billions of people were scattered on a great plain before God's throne.

Most shrank back from the brilliant light before them. But some groups near the front talked heatedly — not with cringing shame, but with belligerence.

'Can God judge us? How can he know about suffering?' snapped a pert young brunette. She ripped open a sleeve to reveal a tattooed number from a Nazi concentration camp. 'We endured terror . . . beatings . . . torture . . . death!'

In another group a Negro boy lowered his collar. 'What about this?' he demanded, showing an ugly rope burn. 'Lynched for no crime but being black!'

In another crowd, a pregnant schoolgirl with sullen eyes. 'Why should I suffer?' she

murmured. 'It wasn't my fault.'

Far out across the plain were hundreds of such groups. Each had a complaint against God for the evil and suffering he permitted in his world. How lucky God was to live in heaven where all was sweetness and light, where there was no weeping or fear, no hunger or hatred. What did God know of all that men had been forced to endure in this world? For God leads a pretty sheltered life, they said.

So each of these groups sent forth their leader, chosen because he had suffered the most. A Jew, a Negro, a person from Hiroshima, a horribly deformed arthritic, a thalidomide child.

In the centre of the plain they consulted with each other. At last they were ready to present their case. It was rather clever.

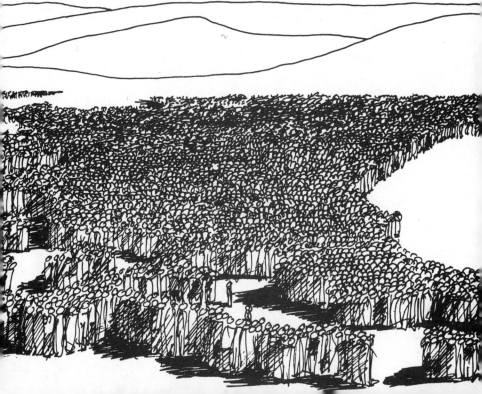

Before God could be qualified to be their judge, he must endure what they had endured. Their decision was that God should be sentenced to live on earth — as a man!

Let him be born a Jew. Let the legitimacy of his birth be doubted.

Give him a work so difficult that even his family will think him out of his mind when he tries to do it. Let him be betrayed by his closest friends. Let him face false charges, be tried by a prejudiced jury and convicted by a cowardly judge. Let him be tortured.

At the last, let him see what it means to be terribly alone. Then let him die. Let him die so that there can be no doubt he died. Let there be a great host of witnesses to verify it.

As each leader announced his portion of
the sentence, loud murmurs of approval
went up from the throng of people
assembled.

When the last had finished pronouncing
sentence, there was a long silence. No one
uttered another word. No one moved.

For suddenly
   all knew
      that

God had already served his sentence.[12]

So . . .

The God of the Bible is supremely qualified to be Judge. As the author and originator of law and justice, he is unequalled in the wisdom and fairness with which he hands down his verdicts. Add to this the fact that he is love and can therefore be relied upon to be utterly merciful, add also that he has committed the task of judgement to Jesus — whose *deity* gives him unique insight into God's character and whose *humanity* unique insight into human nature — and the sum total is that in God we have a Judge *par excellence*.

THE FATHER has given the role of judge to

THE SON

MANKIND is to honour him as Lord and God

The basis of judgement

There are two key issues on which we shall be judged: belief and behaviour.

1. Belief

It is our attitude to Jesus Christ that determines our destiny. God sent him to be the Saviour of the world and to satisfy the demands of justice by his death upon the cross. When we turn to him and accept this for ourselves, he hands down for us the verdict of 'not guilty'. We will not have to wait to hear this at God's judgement seat; it is true for us now. Whatever else the judgement may bring, it will certainly not be condemnation.

Of course, the corollary is that those who refuse Christ's salvation or neglect to accept it are still under judgement — still condemned, still heading for final disaster. Jesus, and what he has done for us, remains the touchstone of judgement.

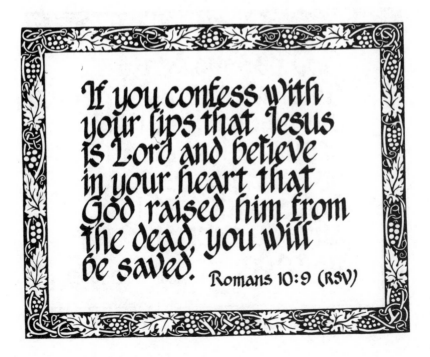

If you confess with your lips that Jesus is Lord and believe in your heart that God raised him from the dead, you will be saved. Romans 10:9 (RSV)

2. Behaviour

The other key issue for judgement is behaviour — our 'works' as the Bible puts it. There is no way that our personal performance could earn us a place in God's kingdom. However our actions are, just the same, very realistic indicators of our inward thoughts and attitudes, a barometer indicating whether our faith in Christ is living and real, or just a sterile, intellectual game.

'Faith works through love', said the apostle Paul. If it is the real thing, faith will express itself in Christian character and activity, especially in concern and compassion for others. In other words how we live as Christians matters a great deal . . . and matters eternally.

We shall enjoy or regret forever the use that we made of our bodies and minds in this world. Even though the final joy of being accepted by God may well swallow up all our regrets, the Bible is warning us that we ought to make every effort to serve God and each other to the best of our ability. We will be judged for it.

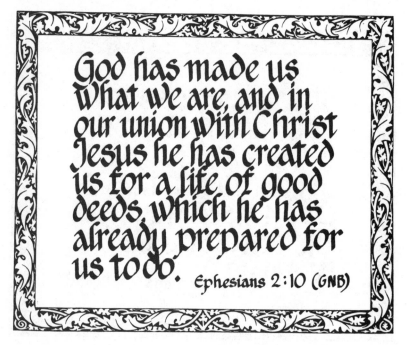

God has made us what we are, and in our union with Christ Jesus he has created us for a life of good deeds, which he has already prepared for us to do.

Ephesians 2:10 (GNB)

Study
Guide

Revelation

1. What are the major obstacles that prevent people from receiving God's communication? Is it because God isn't speaking to them? Compare Romans 1:18-20 and Acts 17:26-28.

2. 'I don't accept the orthodox view of God. I believe he is nature and part of us, rather than a personal God out there in space.'
Does this view come to terms with God's self-revelation? What aspect of the Christian message does it disregard? Read and discuss 1 Corinthians 1:21-25 and 2 Corinthians 5:19.

3. How does special revelation differ from general revelation? What part does Jesus play in it all? Compare John 8:25-30.

4. When Jesus returns, all of humanity will see him (Revelation 1:7). In the meantime, how do we 'see' and 'hear' him? Compare John 14:25-56, John 20:30-31 and Romans 10:17.

5. What advice would you give to the person who sincerely wants to find God, but who wonders if it is all possible? Compare Jeremiah 29:13 and John 7:17.

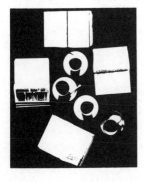

God

1. In Acts 17:22-31, the apostle Paul spoke about God to some highly educated Athenians. What did he say about:

(a) God's name?
(b) God's relationship to the universe?
(c) the origin of the human species?
(d) God's purpose for humanity?
(e) God's attitude to people today?

2. What are some typical contemporary ideas about God that you have encountered? Where do they come from? How do they differ from the Christian understanding of God?

3. Have you found the doctrine of the Trinity a puzzle intellectually? Have you experienced the reality of God as three persons yet one God?

4. Many intelligent people have claimed to have sought God, but have never found him. Why?

Compare Hebrews 11:3 and 6, Isaiah 66:2, Matthew 6:32-34 and 1 John 1:8-9.

5. 'How can we turn our knowledge *about* God into knowledge *of* God? The rule for doing this is demanding, but simple. It is that we turn each truth that we learn *about* God into matter for meditation *before* God, leading to prayer and praise *to* God' (J. I. Packer, *Knowing God*, page 18).

What particular truth about God have you found particularly real in your experience? Describe.

Creation

1. Seven times in Genesis 1 it says 'God saw that it was good', referring to different aspects of his handiwork. What do these statements tell us about God's attitude initially to the created order? What might God say about his creation today?

Compare Genesis 6:5-8 with Romans 8:19-21.

2. If God created the world, what can we conclude about:

(a) his relationship to physical matter?
(b) his relationship to us?
(c) his relationship to time?

3. 'The Bible is not a book of science and therefore does not try to describe the *what* or *how* of creation: What is the structure of a plant cell? How does the kidney work? What is gravity?

It does, however, claim insight into the *who* and *why* of creation: Who made the universe? Why did he make it? Was the world created by pure chance, or was it designed with purpose?

Compare Isaiah 40:28, 42:5-8, 43:10-11 and 15, 45:18. What do these verses say to us about God's character and work as Creator?

4. Many contemporary Christians are puzzled about what is a correct interpretation of Genesis 1 and 2. They agree on the overall meaning of this passage, but stumble on the details.

There seem to be three main schools of thought:

(a) Those who believe that the Bible account is accurate theologically *and* scientifically, especially concerning the origin of the world.

(b) Those who believe that the Bible account is accurate theologically but inaccurate scientifically, using outmoded thought-forms to describe creation.

(c) Those who believe that the Bible account is neither scientific nor unscientific, but non-scientific — that the book of Genesis, as a much more ancient account than modern science, could hardly be speaking the same language as science.

This view holds that the Bible is asking different questions to those of scientific investigation and coming at the truth in a different way.

What is your personal view? Are science and the Bible necessarily incompatible? What particular issues need resolving for you?

5. Why is it that people can 'walk through God's handiwork with never a thought for him'? In practical terms, what does it mean to acknowledge God as Creator?

Compare Ecclesiastes 12:1 and Isaiah 6:1-5.

Conversion

1. The New Testament uses many different metaphors to describe becoming a Christian (experiencing a new birth, being adopted into God's family, being judged 'not guilty').

Which of these most appeals to you? Why? Compare John 3:5-8, Ephesians 1:5-6 and Romans 5:1.

2. Why does 'turning from self' (repentance) not involve destruction of the human personality? How is this process of restoring right relationships a liberating experience?

Compare Mark 1:14-15, Acts 2:37-39 and 1 Thessalonians 1:8-9.

3. What is faith? Is it more a matter of the mind or the heart?

Compare John 20:26-29 with Hebrews 11:1-2 and John 1:11-13.

4. What is the 'quiet revolution' brought about in the life of every Christian? Do the following verses accurately describe your experience?

Compare Galatians 4:6, Ephesians 1:13-14 and 2:17-18, 1 Corinthians 12:13, Romans 8:14-16.

5. Are all conversions dramatic and sudden, or can people grow into faith over a period of time? Describe your own or another's experience to illustrate.

Sanctification

1. The Bible distinguishes between 'works' (self-effort) and 'good works' (what God does in us). How can we tell the difference?

Compare Ephesians 2:8-10 and Colossians 3:17 with John 14:21.

2. What is our part in sanctification and what is God's part? Read Philippians 2:12-13. How can we slide into the old habit of self-effort without realizing it?

3. Think about the description of the Christian life as a partnership between us and God. How does this solve, in part, the traditional conflict between 'free-will' and 'predestination' (God choosing us)?

4. If you had unlimited opportunity, what changes would you make:

(a)   at home?
(b)   at work/your place of study?
(c)   in your leisure activities?
(d)   to your future goals and ambitions?

How do these ideas line up with becoming more Christ-like?

5. Study the qualities of character of those controlled by God's Spirit (Galatians 5:22-23). How are these nine qualities or 'fruit' an antidote to the various manifestations of the self-centred personality (verses 19-21)?

Which fruit is most relevant to your spiritual growth at the present time?

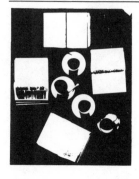

Church

1. Write down, then share with others, three negative 'mental images' about the Christian church that you have heard from people you know.

How accurate are these criticisms?
How can we best remove or answer them?

2. If the church is 'a meeting called by God', how can we enjoy and benefit from it more? What for you are some of the good times you have had in church?

3. What in concrete terms does it mean to 'invest our lives in others'? In what practical ways can this be done through our local church? Should we limit ourselves to this avenue?

4. How should 'the minister' in a local church assist the membership 'in the ministry'. What are some of the factors or reasons preventing this from happening?

5. What is the connection between formal church worship and worship as part of our everyday life?

What makes worship 'come alive' for you?

Prayer

1. What obstacles do you find are the key ones when you come to pray? In what ways could they be overcome?

2. Why do you think God sometimes makes us wait for answers to our prayers? How do you reconcile this with Jesus' promise in Luke 11:9-10 and John 14:13-14?

3. Study the Lord's Prayer (Matthew 6:9-13). Do you keep to the priorities laid down by Jesus: God's work, our needs?

What does it mean for God to 'lead us not into temptation'? How is God's testing (James 1:2-3, 1 Peter 1:6-7, Hebrews 12:5-6) different from Satan's tempting (Job 1:8-12, Mark 1:13, James 1:13-14)?

Will God always protect us from temptation?

Compare 1 Corinthians 10:13.

4. Think about the 'prepositions' of prayer: we pray *to* God *through* Christ *by* the Holy Spirit. What is the role of each person of the Trinity in prayer? What is our part in it?

Compare Revelation 8:3-4, Hebrews 4:14-16 and Romans 8:26-27.

5. Should we plan to pray, or simply pray when we feel like it?

Share with others some practical pointers that have helped you be better organized for prayer. What specific procedures work for you?

Judgement

1. How do you reconcile the two aspects of God's character: his love, his justice? Is judgement inevitable? What prevents God from acting against mankind's universal rebellion now?

Compare Acts 17:30-31, Romans 10:12-13, 2 Corinthians 5:10 and Hebrews 9:27.

2. Realizing the sentimental climate of modern society, in what ways can we introduce the idea of judgement to people? What recent historical event or contemporary situation illustrates its inevitability?

3. What are some key contemporary moral issues facing:

(a)   us individually?
(b)   society at large?
How will Jesus judge them?

4. What is the connection between belief and behaviour? Can we be successful publicly, yet bankrupt morally and spiritually?

5. How can we avoid a judgemental spirit, while maintaining a strong belief in God's right to be judge? Compare 1 Corinthians 4:5 and Romans 2:1-5.

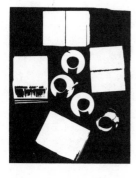

End notes:

[1]Adapted from Simon Jenkins, 'Like . . .', *Rhinoceros* (London: Fool Press, n.d.)
[2]J. I. Packer, *Evangelism and the Sovereignty of God* (IVP), pp. 18-19
[3]Bob Dylan quoted by Robert Hilburn, "Dylan: 'I Learned That Jesus Is Real
  and I Wanted That,' " *Los Angeles Times,* Calendar, 23 November 1980, p. 8
[4]John Wesley, *Journals* (Epworth Press), entry for 24 May, 1738
[5]Sir Wilfred Grenfell, *The Story of a Labrador Doctor* (Hodder & Stoughton), p. 30
[6]A. J. Appasamy, *Sundar Singh* (Lutterworth), p. 21
[7]C. S. Lewis, *Surprised by Joy* (Fontana), pp. 182-183 and 189
[8]Malcolm Muggeridge, 'Living through an Apocalypse', from *Let the Earth Hear
  His Voice:* International Congress on World Evangelization, Lausanne, Switzerland
  (World Wide Publications), p. 449
[9]Charles Colson, *Born Again* (Hodder & Stoughton), pp. 129-130
[10]William Temple, *Readings in St John's Gospel* (MacMillan), p. 68
[11]C. S. Lewis, *Reflections on the Psalms* (Fontana), p. 80
[12]'The Long Silence', quoted by Stephen Travis, *The Jesus Hope* (IVP), p. 61

Photos:

Russell Conway (p. 89), Mike Elkner (pp. 75, 119 and 120), John Morey
(pp. 129 and 130), John Waterhouse (p. 13), Jim Whitmer (pp. 17, 62, 73, 116),
sculpture 'Christ Crucified' by Helen Huntington Jennings from Coventry Cathedral,
UK (p. 140)